Cindy

PUMPKINS

HARVEST TO HOME

Lynn M. Stone

Rourke Publishing LLC

Ve   2964

www.rourkepublishing.com

PHOTO CREDITS:
All photos © Lynn M. Stone except p. 13 courtesy of Nestle Food Company and p. 10 © William Allen

EDITORIAL SERVICES:
Pamela Schroeder

Library of Congress Cataloging-in-Publication Data

Stone, Lynn M.
    Pumpkins / Lynn M. Stone.
        p. cm. — (Harvest to home)
    ISBN 1-58952-130-7
    1. Pumpkin—Juvenile literature. [1. Pumpkin] I. Title

SB347.S76 2001
635'.62—dc21   2001031663

Printed in the USA

TABLE OF CONTENTS

Pumpkins   5

Growing Pumpkins   14

Harvesting Pumpkins   20

Glossary   23

Index   24

Further Reading/Websites to Visit   24

PUMPKINS

Autumn comes each year with colorful leaves, frosty nights, and football. It also brings pumpkins!

Pumpkins are the best known of autumn vegetables. They're used as jack-o-lanterns, tasty filling in pies, and Halloween decorations. Pumpkins are also used in bread, soup, cake, and animal feeds. Dried and salted pumpkin seeds are a favorite American snack.

Straight from the can, this pumpkin "paste" will be used in pumpkin pie.

Pumpkins are like squash. Most pumpkins are orange or yellowish. Some are nearly white.

A pumpkin may be oval-shaped like an egg or it may be as round as a basketball.

Some pumpkins are about the size of basketballs. But all pumpkins are not alike. The pumpkins used for pie filling are a different **variety** than the pumpkins used for jack-o-lanterns.

Most pumpkins are bright orange, but some are white, tan, or yellow.

Pumpkins come in many varieties. The varieties are different sizes, colors, and shapes.

Most pumpkins weigh between 15 and 30 pounds (7 and 14 kilograms). A few weigh 100 pounds (45 kg) or more. But the Atlantic giant pumpkin is in a class of its own. This garden monster can grow to more than 1,000 pounds (455 kg). The record Atlantic giant, grown in Ohio, weighed more than 1,100 pounds (500 kg)!

Pumpkins come in different sizes and shapes.

If pumpkins were solid, they would be even heavier. But inside a pumpkin's hard "shell" is an airy center. People who make jack-o-lanterns know that the inside of a pumpkin is almost hollow. Thump on a pumpkin. You'll hear a sound like rapping on a hollow tree.

Most of a pumpkin's weight is in its meaty shell. The pumpkin's center has seeds and soft, wet, stringy material called **pulp**. It's easy to cut away the pulp and seeds.

A jack-o-lantern carver slices through the meaty pumpkin shell and into the airy center.

Pumpkins are great autumn decorations—and heads for straw dummies!

Pumpkins are cleaned, sliced, heated, and crushed before they are packed into cans as pumpkin paste.

GROWING PUMPKINS

Pumpkins grow all over the United States and southern Canada. People plant them in home gardens as well as in huge, open fields, called pumpkin patches.

Pumpkins grow from seeds that are usually planted between April 25 and May 25. Pumpkin seeds take about 120 days to become full-grown pumpkins.

This pumpkin patch is growing jack-o-lantern pumpkins.

Farmers with large pumpkin fields plant their seeds with a tractor and corn planter. The corn planter is a machine that plants many seeds at a time.

Most kinds of pumpkins grow on long vines that stretch and curl along the ground. The young vines have leaves and flowers. The flowers slowly die but tiny new pumpkins take their place—with the help of bees.

Young, growing pumpkins are green until they ripen in late summer and early fall.

Pumpkin plants need bees to make pumpkins. Flowers make a powder-like material called **pollen**. Pollen from one flower must reach pollen from another for pumpkins to begin growing. Bees love pollen, so they land on one flower, then another. Pollen that sticks to the bees' legs and bodies rubs off on the next flower. In that way, bees carry pollen from flower to flower.

As pumpkins grow, farmers must be sure that they have enough water. Farmers with large crops may **irrigate** their fields.

Yellow grains of pollen in the flowers of pumpkin plants attract bees.

HARVESTING PUMPKINS

Pumpkins are **harvested** from the last week of August into October. Visitors to pumpkin farms can often pick their own pumpkins. Machines pulled by tractors harvest pumpkins in the fields. One machine cuts pumpkins from their vines. Another scoops them onto a truck.

Picking your own pumpkin is a fall treat.

Pie pumpkins are **processed** in pumpkin factories. Machines wash and slice pumpkins. They remove, dry, and bag the pumpkin seeds. Other machines chop pumpkin shells into small pieces for cooking. Machines squeeze water from the pumpkin pulp. Pumpkin pulp is scraped away from the skin, crushed into pumpkin paste and put into cans.

GLOSSARY

harvested (HAR ves ted) — gathered, as with a crop

irrigate (IR eh gayt) — to bring water to crops

pollen (PAHL en) — grains of powder-like material made by flowers and used in the making of new flowers

processed (PRAHS est) — having been changed through a planned series of steps

pulp (PULP) — the soft, moist part of some fruits and vegetables

variety (veh RY eh tee) — a somewhat different type of the same basic fruit or vegetable

INDEX

Atlantic giant   9
bees   16, 19
corn planter   16
factories   22
farmers   16, 19
harvest   20
jack-o-lanterns   5, 6, 11

paste   22
pie   5, 22
pollen   19
pulp   11, 22
pumpkin patch   14
seeds   5, 11, 14, 16, 22
vines   16, 20

Further Reading

Gibbons, Gail. *The Pumpkin Book*. Holiday House, 2000
Levenson, George. and Thaler, Shmuel (illustrator). *Pumpkin Circle: The Story of a Garden.* Tricycle Press, 1999.

Websites To Visit

www.pumpkinnook.com
www.backyardgardener.com

About The Author

Lynn Stone is the author of more than 400 children's books. He is a talented natural history photographer as well. Lynn, a former teacher, travels worldwide to photograph wildlife in its natural habitat.